Who, Me Lead a Group?

Jean Illsley Clarke

D0668727

Parenting Press, Inc.
Seattle, Washington

To my father
Harry A. Illsley,
who taught me how to work with groups
years before I learned that big words
like group process existed

Text and illustrations copyright © 1984
by Jean Illsley Clarke
Published in 1998 by Parenting Press, Inc.,
Seattle, Washington

Illustrations by Dean Vietor

Library of Congress Cataloging-in-Publication Data
Clarke, Jean Illsley, 1925-
    Who, me lead a group? / Jean Illsley Clarke.
        p.   cm.
    Originally published: Minneapolis, Minn. : Winston
        Press, c1984.
    Includes bibliographical references and index.
    ISBN 1-884734-41-3 (pbk.)
    1. Leadership.   I. Title.
    HD57.7.C54 1998
    374'.2'019--dc21   98-12096

Parenting Press, Inc.
P.O. Box 75267
Seattle, Washington 98125

ACKNOWLEDGMENTS

For ideas and challenges .... Deane Gradous

For searching questions .... Sally Dierks

For encouragement to frame the
material about the four kinds of
groups .... Wayne Paulson

For probing reading .... Wade Clarke,
Sandra Sittko,
Cheryl
Kirchhoff,
Kathleen Bliven

For designing the checklist for
leadership skills .... Annette Pattie

For experience .... all of the people
with whom I
have learned in
groups

I thank you!

CONTENTS

HOW TO START

So you are going to lead a group? Fine. If you have led groups, you will find that this book addresses, perhaps in new ways, many things you have already experienced. If you are about to lead your first group, you will notice that the book is organized around ten questions. These are the questions that people frequently ask as they prepare to lead groups. I suggest that you read quickly through the first nine questions (see pp. iv-vi). No doubt you will realize how much you already know about leading groups.

The tenth question, "How Do I Plan My Meeting?", offers help in preparing for a specific group meeting. As you make your plans, you can look back to earlier questions and reread sections that will help you clarify what you need to do.

At the end of the meeting-planning section are two checklists for leadership evaluation. One checklist is organized around leadership skills; the second checklist is designed to follow the structure of the meeting plans. Choose one to help you identify things you did well and ways you can improve your leadership of future events.

Go ahead, make your plans, and lead your group. If you are a beginner, remember that the way to get started is to start. If you are an accomplished leader, use the questions to help you focus on skills that need improvement.

I hope that you enjoy *Who, Me Lead a Group?* and find it helpful. Feel free to write in the book.

Add your own ideas and experiences, star ideas for future growth, disagree, write notes to yourself. The book is based on the experience and research of many leaders, but it will only be useful to you when you make it your own.

Four Types of Groups

As you read, you can be thinking about what kind of group you are going to be leading. There are four general types of learning groups:

Discovery groups
Sharing groups
Skill-building or task groups
Planning groups

Some leadership techniques work well in all four types of groups, but there are specific areas in which different techniques are appropriate. For example, methods of writing behavioral goals for the four groups differ significantly. These differences will be explained and illustrated throughout the book with examples for each of the four types of groups. The group types will be identified by the symbols that are listed above.

Each of the four types of groups has a different focus or emphasis.

 Discovery groups focus on raising awareness of some kind. The emphasis is often on internal and personal aspects.

 Sharing and support groups provide an opportunity for people to exchange something of value. The emphasis is on the individual's interactions with other persons.

Skill-building or task groups center on the skill or product that the person or group is to acquire or produce. The members of the group concentrate on learning a skill and/or producing a product.

Planning groups focus on designing a plan that is future-oriented. The goal is to produce a specific recommendation or blueprint for action.

Let us compare how the activities of the four groups would differ if they were all organized around the same topic. For example, think about how the groups would differ if each were about music. The same group of people could come together:

in a discovery group designed to help each person get more pleasure from listening to classical music. Group name: "Enjoying Classical Music."

in a sharing group to play instruments and sing together just for fun. Group name: "The Joyful Noise Bunch."

in a task group to practice for a band concert to be given at the fourth-of-July community celebration. Group name:

"Minnetonka City Band."

in a skill-building group to increase the individual's ability to sightread and the group's ability to sing difficult harmonies. Group name: "Advanced Chorus."

in a planning group to design the calendar of concerts and parties for the coming year.

Group name: "Orchestra Events Committee."

Before we talk about how a specific group can fall into more than one category, let us expand on each of the four group types. Read the description of each type of group and the list of examples on the following pages. Choose a title that could be of interest to you from each list of examples. Decide what the major activities for the group you chose might be, and write those activities in the space available on those pages.

Discovery groups

Discovery groups focus on self-awareness or on increasing an awareness of each individual's relationship to a special group, issue, possibility, or problem. The focus of such a group may be on knowledge, values, or both.

Examples:

Title

"My Family Myths and Me"

"Nuclear Arms Study Group"

"The Lessons of the Book of Job for My Life"

"Enjoying Classical Music"

"Styles of Child Rearing"

"The Role of OSHA in Industrial Safety and
Efficiency"

"Clothes Make the Person"

"Can Quality Circles Help Your Company?"

Activity

-I will identify several Myths that were
strong in my family & how I follow them.

-I will learn about many facets of the
nuclear arms race -- safety, costs, politics.

Sharing groups

 Sharing (and support) groups are designed to help members exchange information, feelings, hopes, grief, concerns.

Examples:

Title

"Symposium on Worker Safety"

"How Nuclear Power Affects Our Daily Lives"

"Marriage Encounter"

"Grief Support Group"

"Bible Discussion Group"

"Parent Support Group"

"Alcoholics Anonymous"

"A Workshop for Managers: What Makes Your Quality Circles Work?"

Activity

—I will explain ways our business promotes worker safety + I will listen to what others do.

—I will get new info on effects of nuclear power. I will discuss with other people what the implications of use of nuclear power are for our lives

Skill-building groups

 Skill-building (or task) groups are intended to help the members complete specific tasks or increase job, recreational, physical, mental, spiritual, personal, interpersonal, or group skills.

Examples:

Title

"Couple Communication"

"How to Influence Your Legislators"

"The Steps in Grieving"

"How to Lead a Junior-High Church Group"

"Systematic Training for Effective Parenting"

"How to Design a Safe Environment for Day Care"

"Sew a Weekend Travel Wardrobe"

"Introducing Quality Circles in Your Business: A Six-Step Method"

Activity

—I will identify and practice new ways of communicating with another person.

—I will learn methods people use to influence legislators & will use several of them.

Planning groups

The members of planning groups meet to plan for the future. Anything from one event for a single individual to the next thirty years for a nation can be explored by a planning group. You may be familiar with these groups as boards, task forces, or committees.

Examples:

Title

"Safety Recommendation Committee"

"The Ad Hoc Committee on Nuclear Power"

"Jewish Community Center Long-Range Planning
   Committee"

"Task Force on Finding Ways Our School Can
   Identify and Support Children of Divorce"

"Parish Education Committee"

"Governor's Task Force on Families"

"Advisory Board"

"Executive Planning Board"

Activity

-We will review safety codes for the industry.

We will assess safety practice & make recommendations.

-We will assess current use of nuclear power in

the state as it relates to energy needs. We will

make a list of recommendations on role of power

during the future.

_____

_____

_____

As time passes, some groups may move from one category to another. A group on "The Power of the Media" could ⟨DISCOVERY⟩ raise awareness of current media practices, ⟨SHARING⟩ share responses to different media approaches, ⟨SKILL BUILDING⟩ learn how to design a media presentation, and ⟨PLANNING⟩ plan ways to use media for a specific purpose. Such a group would have moved through all four categories.

Other groups will fall into two or three categories at the same time. For example, groups studying *Self-Esteem: A Family Affair*[1] ⟨DISCOVERY⟩ increase their awareness of their own attitudes and behavior, ⟨SHARING⟩ find out what other parents think, and ⟨SKILL BUILDING⟩ practice parenting skills at each meeting.

Remember that your group is important, no matter what its purpose or its size. Go ahead. Explore the book and develop your plans. Good luck to you as you learn more about leading groups—and may your leadership be empowered and your success abundant.

QUESTION 1

What Are the Qualities of an Effective Leader of Adult Learning Groups?

Warmth, indirectness, cognitive organization, and enthusiasm are four qualities that are found in effective leaders of adult groups.[2] Ask yourself how much of each of these qualities you already possess.

1. *Warmth.*

   Effective leaders:
   - speak well of people.
   - tend to like and trust rather than fear other people.
   - establish warm relationships with people.

2. *Indirectness.*

   Effective leaders:
   - let people discover things for themselves.
   - are willing to refrain from telling everything they know, even when it would be "good for people." Researcher Allan Tough found that learners preferred helpers who offered helpful resources rather than "answers."[3]

3. *Cognitive organization.*

   Effective leaders:
   - have clear behavioral objectives in mind.
   - divide learning into orderly steps.

- have knowledge well-categorized so that they can offer appropriate data in response to questions.
- are clear about what they know and what they don't know.
- are willing to say they do not know and do not pretend when they are in doubt.

4. *Enthusiasm.*

   Effective leaders:
   - feel enthusiastic about people.
   - are enthusiastic about the subject matter.

The combination of these qualities is a powerful force for learning. The warmth gives people permission to learn; the indirectness offers people the protection they need to discover their own learnings; and the cognitive organization and enthusiasm are reflections of potent leadership.

Using the scales on p. 16, rate yourself by circling a number for each of these qualities. When you have finished reading this book, return to this section and rate yourself again. You may discover that you already have more leadership skills than you thought you had. When you rate yourself after you lead several meetings, you may find that you have sharpened your leadership skills considerably.

WARMTH

| 10 | 9 | 8 | 7 | 6 | 5 | 4 | 3 | 2 | 1 |

warm, open,
friendly

cold,
closed

INDIRECTNESS

| 10 | 9 | 8 | 7 | 6 | 5 | 4 | 3 | 2 | 1 |

helpful in allowing
people to discover
for themselves

eager to tell
everything I
know

COGNITIVE ORGANIZATION

| 10 | 9 | 8 | 7 | 6 | 5 | 4 | 3 | 2 | 1 |

clear about goals,
well-organized,
willing to
say "I don't know"

disorganized,
rambling,
unable to
complete things

ENTHUSIASM

| 10 | 9 | 8 | 7 | 6 | 5 | 4 | 3 | 2 | 1 |

positive about subject
matter and people,
expressive

flat,
passive, or
cynical

You may already possess an abundance of each of these qualities. If not, you can generate your own warmth and enthusiasm. *Who, Me Lead a Group?* can help you to sharpen your organizational skills and to improve your ability to lead indirectly.

QUESTION 2

How Do Adults Learn, and How Can I Facilitate Adult Learning Groups?

What Motivates Adults to Learn?

Adults who want to learn are motivated in either a general or a specific way. A vague dissatisfaction and a desire to do something better are examples of general motivations. People with general motivation say things such as:

"I wish I understood myself better."

"I just want to talk with some other people."

"I would like to learn to communicate better."

"I keep wondering where this group is going."

Specific motivations come from internal pressure generated by a specific life situation. Examples of specific motivation are:

"Will this program help me understand what the threat of nuclear war means to me and my family?"

"I'm upset because my spouse and I don't agree on how to handle our teenager who got a DWI ticket. Are there any parents in this group who have solved that problem?"

"I want to know how to speak Spanish before my trip to Mexico."

"Our committee has to come up with a plan for moving into the international market, but I only know the domestic market."

Sometimes the motivation to learn comes from outside the learner. The need for academic certification or pressure from a superior to change one's behavior are good examples. People who come to meetings because they are motivated by outside pressure can be resistant learners. One way for the leader to lessen this resistance is to take the time to help people discover how the learning experience can directly benefit them. Involve them in the goal-setting process. Challenge them to find a way that

the group meeting can benefit them *even though* it is
required.

What Are the Steps in Adults' Learning Process?

STEP 1: Where Adults Get Information
Once motivated to begin working toward a learning
goal, adults seek information or help at some time.
Some people turn to friends or co-workers, some go
to the library or find other sources of written material, some use television or other media sources, and
some attend meetings in order to learn. Adults who
attend meetings often expect:
- to learn useful concepts and skills offered by the
  leader.
- to be offered visual helps such as books, charts,
  films.
- to benefit from the collective experience of other
  people in the group.

   Adult learners prefer to be in charge of their own
learning. So it is important for the leader to be a
facilitator, whose role is:
- to present material and then leave the decision about
  the materials and the life application up to the
  learners.
- to be sure that the visual material is available, clear,
  and readable.
- to structure ways in which the learners can tap the
  resources of other people in the group.

STEP 2: How Adults Organize Learning Material

Adults organize new information as they collect it, but not all of them organize it in the same way. Some of them prefer to get an overview of the material— a big picture—or an abstract theory, and then see where various parts or the concrete experiences fit in. Other adults organize learning material by searching about for bits and pieces, or even large chunks, from which to create their own view of the big picture. Many adults like a quick view of the big picture or the general theory, immediately followed by some parts, or some concrete experiences, to start fitting into it.

The people who need the big picture first are often very goal-oriented. They are uncomfortable when asked to do something unless there is an explanation first indicating how the activity contributes to the larger goal. These people like to hear the abstract theory before the direct experience that illustrates it. They prefer to learn the basic principle and *then* see how it applies. Such adults are eager to get a feeling for the whole project before they start work on an individual task. Not only do they want to know the purpose of the learning, but they feel uncomfortable if they do not know what content and methods will be used. They say things like:

- "I really don't get it."
- "I don't know what you are driving at."
- "I don't understand how this fits."
- "What does this have to do with me?"
- "I don't see why you are doing this."

It is as if they are not part of the learning, as if something is happening *to* them. If these adults don't get the structure they need in order to become part of the learning process, they are apt to leave.

Once these people have the big picture, they join the learning process and make judgments about how individual pieces fit into the overall scheme. Then they say things like:

- "I see how that fits within the framework you described."
- "I think this piece makes more sense if we use it this way."
- "I have an idea that relates to our topic."

Now they are in charge of their learning and are helping to make things happen.

People in the second category, those who like to build from small pieces, organize their learning experiences in a different way. They like to see a play before reading a review that summarizes the plot; they prefer to hear a story from the beginning without being told the ending ahead of time. These people are comfortable learning each individual step of the dance and then putting it all together. They start to assemble a toy before they read the directions. They enjoy taking a variety of direct experiences and combining them to see if they make a meaningful whole.

When these people aren't offered enough separate pieces or concrete experiences, they say things like:

- "That wasn't a good meeting—too much lecture."
- "The explanation was too long."
- "I like it better when we jump right in and do things."
- "Too boring."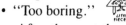

After they get the pieces they need, they regain their enthusiasm and make remarks such as:

- "This is beginning to fit together for me."
- "I like how this builds on what we did at the last meeting."
- "Have you noticed how these things connect?"

- "I saw something on TV that relates to one of the things we did in the group."

Now these adults are in control of their learning and are contributing to the process.

Most groups include some people who want to see the big picture from the beginning, some people who want to build the big picture for themselves, and some people who want some of both. Early in each meeting be sure to:

- state the goals or review the big picture clearly and quickly.
- present at least one separate piece of information or one specific example.

Examples:

"The Role of Rituals in Celebrating Life's Passages"

"Today we will be listing the life passages that can be celebrated by rituals and personally evaluating some of our experiences with those marker events. To start, will each of you remember one ritual or marker event that was satisfying for you? Then think about whether there was some passage, some event, that you would have liked to celebrate, but didn't."

"The Importance of Rituals in Building Strong Family Life"

"We have already shared thoughts about the usual rituals that mark birth, marriage, and death. Today we will share ideas about how to celebrate growth or mark developmental stages in families. To start, will each of you think about how your family marked your entrance into adolescence? Share that information with your partner and also indicate whether you want to celebrate your child's pubescence in the same way."

"Family Meeting"

"This is our first Christmas holiday since the death of our last grandparent. Before we make our plans for this holiday, let's each think of one Christmas activity we especially liked to do with Grandpa and Grandma; then we can talk about how to handle each of these activities this year."

"Task Force on the Role of Rituals in a Changing Church"

"We have already reviewed our rituals for the celebration of birth, marriage, and death. Our task for today is to consider the role of confirmation. It is one mark of growing up. Before we start our discussion, will each of you pause and think back to your early adolescence? What was the most meaningful marker or rite of passage for you? Was it connected with the church?"

There is an important reason for the leader to include both theory and experience in each learning segment of a meeting. People do not use abstract theory to change behavior until they translate the theory into concrete experience. Conversely, learning from one concrete experience is not transferred to another experience until the learning has been related to some abstract theory or made symbolic.

For example, the phrase "love for all human-kind" is a symbol. This phrase represents an abstract theory. A person who writes about the importance of love for all humankind (abstract) and beats a four-year-old who interrupts his writing process (concrete) hasn't connected the symbols with the experience. Not until the person has connected those symbols with some concrete love experiences (such as willingly caring for a child or experiencing unexpected help from a stranger) can he start to behave in ways that express love for all humankind. On the other hand, an adult who devotes time to providing tender, loving nurturing for one child (concrete) and sees no need to spend tax dollars for a traffic light at a hazardous school crossing to protect many children (abstract) hasn't connected the isolated concrete experience of expressing love for a child with the theory of love of children.

Therefore, in order to honor the need for concrete experiences and for abstract theory, it is important at every meeting for the leader to:

- present abstract theories and concepts clearly.
- point out how theory relates to the overall goals.
- include specific activities that illustrate concrete ways in which the theories can be experienced and evaluated in the daily context.
- help people to generalize from specific, concrete experiences to the abstract.

Examples:

 The music-theory lecture on tonal arrangements in Byzantine music (abstract) is more meaningful if snatches of music are played (concrete) that illustrate the various points.

The grief support group accepts and supports a new member's sighs and tears (concrete). Group members also teach him about the stages of grief that people usually go through (abstract).

The communication-skills teacher talks about the importance of reflective listening in communication (abstract). Then she divides people into small groups to practice reflective listening and identify specific instances in which accurate reflective listening would speed problem resolution (concrete).

The safety-recommendation committee designs a recommended policy statement on safety (abstract) and lists specific recommendations for each area of the building (concrete).

STEP 3: How Adults Take in Information

As a leader, you are now ready to present abstract theories and concrete experiences. How will you do that?

Adults seem to acquire most of their information in four ways: through their eyes, their ears, their bodies, and their intuition. Some adults use all four methods.

Intuition is the act of knowing something without being sure how we know it. Learners are responsible for using their own intuition. But group leaders are responsible for providing information for the eyes, the ears, and the body to use.

Some people have a strong preference for taking information in through their eyes, or visually. They like to read, to look at people when they talk, to see pictures, diagrams, and charts, to watch films. They turn on the light before they answer the phone. Visual people say things like:

- "I'll look into it."
- "Show me what you want me to do."
- "Look, I already told you what I want."
- "Are you beginning to see the light?"
- "I get the picture."

Other people prefer to collect information through their ears, or audibly. They would rather listen to the news on the radio than look at the newspaper. They are uncomfortable when background noise interferes with the auditory cues they are accustomed to hearing. Auditory people listen to a story rather than read it and use cassettes or radios to collect information while driving. They would prefer verbal directions to a map or road signs. They say things like:

- "I hear you."
- "Tell you what I'll do."
- "Lend me your ear."
- "Now listen, I'm telling you what I want."
- "That's music to my ears."

Some adults learn best with their bodies, or kinesthetically. They like to "walk through things." They are impatient with lectures, and they move their toes and their fingers while they think. These people like to go for long walks to think things over, or they make decisions while jogging. While they think, they may walk purposefully around a room in a way that is different from anxious pacing. They say things like:

- "I'll run through some possible solutions in my mind."
- "Let's find out if anyone came up with a new solution."
- "I've been kicking that idea around."
- "I think I have a handle on it now."
- "She is getting it together."

Taste and smell are important ways that people can collect information, but these methods are often discounted or ignored when planning group learning experiences—except when they relate to food or beverages. How much do you think the learning in a group is affected if the room smells fresh instead of musty? or if it has the lingering odor of lilacs instead of yesterday's cigar butts?

Many learners do not depend on one sense but prefer to use all of their senses, in addition to their intuition, to collect information. Even people with a very strong sense preference use the other senses in a secondary way.

One way to be sure you are appealing to a variety of senses is to analyze learning activities on a checklist. (For an example, see pp. 30-31. This list includes listening, looking, talking, writing or drawing, moving or role playing, and interacting in groups.) List each separate step in your total presentation and check the sensory activities it appeals to. After you lead your meeting, compare activities that rated several checks with those that received one or two, and note which activities got the best response from your group.

HOW MANY SENSES?

1. *Opening exercise* ✓ ✓

2. *Brainstorming* ✓ ✓

3. *Suggestion circle* ✓

4.

5.

6.

7.

8.

9.

10.

11.

12.

(Turn to p. 108 for a blank copy of this form.)

HOW MANY SENSES?

SPEAK

WRITE

MOVE

INTERACT

SPEAK	WRITE	MOVE	INTERACT
✓	✓		✓
✓	✓		✓
✓			✓

Most learners appreciate some variety in the way material is presented. Have you ever struggled to stay awake through a long slide presentation, slide after slide passing by while the same monotonous voice drones on and on? Yes, a slide show is both auditory and visual, but many adults find their attention straying after about twelve minutes of any presentation. Plan to change your methods of presentation often.

So what is the leader's responsibility to provide for the different ways that adults take in information? A leader should remember that no matter what the personal learning-style preferences are:

- Attractive, readable visuals are important.
- Clear, spoken messages are important.
- Learning exercises that involve moving the body are important.
- Adequate ventilation and comfortable temperature are important.

STEP 4: How Adults Start to Make Changes in Their Lives

When people start to make changes in some area of their lives, they may begin by:

- changing the way they talk about it.
- changing their attitude toward it.
- changing how they act, or raising their skill level.
- altering an underlying decision or value about it.

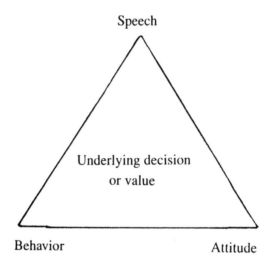

Think about which position you take on the triangle when you start to make a change. Remember that if a change is started at any point and maintained conscientiously and consistently over time, adjustments in the other positions will follow. Be aware that each of these positions can be an effective place to start to change, and do not expect to see only one pattern of change in your group(s).

Examples:

[DISCOVERY] Let us say that you are leading a group on violence in society, and Julia has announced that she is going to stop spanking her child as a method of discipline. Julia can start to make this change in her life by altering her words, her attitudes, her behavior, or her basic decision.

Julia may take the first step by changing the way she *speaks* about her child. She will say, "Logan needs discipline," instead of "Logan needs a spanking." Or Julia could take the first step by changing her *behavior*. When she feels like spanking Logan, she will move him off to sit in the corner instead.

She could examine her concept of discipline and change her *attitude* from a flippant "Spare the rod and spoil the child" to a thoughtful "It is my responsibility to socialize my child without using violence."

Julia may even change an *underlying decision*. Suppose, for example, she had accepted the idea that women are powerless. She, therefore, did not expect and demand certain behaviors from Logan, but let him do whatever he wanted. When his behavior became intolerable to her, she hit him. After Julia changes her belief about herself and claims her power and her ability to model, she expects and demands appropriate social behavior. Logan's behavior improves so that she no longer finds it intolerable and, therefore, she doesn't spank.

[SHARING] You are leading a support group on career changes. Craig, a group member, has decided to improve his position at work. He may start by changing his *words* from "I don't know how to do that'' to ''Where can I learn how to do that?'' He may begin by checking out his *assumption* that no one at work cares if he progresses and then exchange his defeatist *attitude* for one that expects some support.

Craig could enroll in a class to improve his skills *(behavior)*. Or he could examine his *underlying belief* about himself and whether he deserves a job in which he can expect and achieve promotions.

[SKILL BUILDING] You are leading a series of classes for small business owners on the subject of motivating employees. Clara starts to improve her motivation skills by listening to other employers and reading books on the topic. She examines her own *attitude* toward it. John is changing the way he *talks* to his employees. Jeff is rethinking his *underlying beliefs* as to whether one person really can motivate another, and Phyllis announces that she gave everyone a raise *(behavior)* to see if that will motivate workers to produce more.

[PLANNING] You are the chair of your church's long-range planning committee. The board asked you to think about long-range plans but did not seem interested in what the plans will be or when they will be ready. You want to start by scheduling regular *discussions* with the board to talk about new ways for this church to plan for the future. Fred wants to start *making a plan* immediately. Julie thinks the committee should address the idea of educating the congregation, as some members have a negative *attitude* toward planning. Richard is busy thinking about whether this planning idea is too secular. Perhaps the church should trust in God's plan. He is considering his *underlying value*.

As a leader, be sure to notice and reward each of the ways that people start their changes.

STEP 5: How Adults Look, Act, and Sound While They Are Learning New Skills

While they are making changes and practicing new skills, many adults look and feel awkward. As they try out and refine a new skill, they gradually become graceful. A few adults seem to burst forth with new behavior as suddenly as if they put on a new hat and the hat changed the way they walked. Often those people are not exhibiting behavior that they decided to change only a minute ago, but are showing the results of a period of thought, decision-making, or practice in fantasy. It is as if they got through the awkward period internally or in private.

Probably all adults experience some awkwardness while learning a new skill, just as children do. Some people find learning new skills exciting and don't mind the clumsiness. Others equate awkwardness with insincerity and feel tempted to stop practicing the new behavior. They excuse their lack of willingness to change with statements like:

"I want to give more compliments, but I just didn't sound sincere; so I stopped doing it. I'm afraid my voice sounds phony."

"I'm not used to talking about feelings and I think it sounds silly. Did you see the ball game?"

"I have practiced this seventeen times and I don't think I'll ever get it right."

"I don't think we can make a plan that will work. How do we know what will have happened a year from now?"

It is important for the leader to create a climate in the meetings where:

- People get support for achievement.
- It is safe for people to practice even when they are uncomfortable.
- It is safe for people to be or feel awkward.
- It is safe for people to try out a new behavior before they choose to keep or discard it.

QUESTION 3

How Do I Open the Meeting, and How Important Is Opening?

How do you open the meeting? Say, "Hello, let's get started," and start—on time. *Even* if everyone is not there. If you have to do some kind of book-keeping (taking down names and addresses or col-lecting money), the way in which you do it sets the tone for the workshop; so be fully there—talk with people, let them know you. Many people make last-ing judgments about a class or workshop based on how the leader behaves during the first three min-utes; remember that your first three minutes start when people walk through the door.

If yours is a group in which you expect people to talk with each other, arrange the chairs in a circle (if at all possible). Names are an important way to encourage communication. Unless you are sure everyone knows everyone else, give people name tags— and remember to wear one yourself.

Clear, colorful, readable posters are reassuring to those who rely on visuals. Be sure the words can be read from across the room.

It is all right to start before everyone has arrived. You discount the people who came on time if you wait. Greet latecomers, but don't make a fuss over them. Expect them to slide into the activities and find a quiet way to catch up with what they've missed.

The opening activity for each meeting should signal both the content and process of the meeting. If you lecture for the first fifteen minutes, people will expect you to do lots of talking. If you plan to have them discuss, then be sure that they talk with another person within the first twelve minutes.

Example:

Your group is studying traditions. As an opening exercise, you could ask each person to:

• Choose a partner.
• Make a name tag for that person.
• Ask the partner to tell about one or two family traditions remembered as favorites from childhood.

If it is a support or sharing group, after about five minutes you could ask each person to introduce a partner and tell the group about the partner's favorite tradition. Or you could ask for awarenesses in a discovery group, or learnings in a skill or task group.

In many religious, civic, and fraternal groups, a regular opening ritual including personal greetings and a group reading or prayer serves these opening functions.

What Are the Qualities of a Good Opening Activity?

1. Starts on time.
2. Moves; has high energy, quickness.
3. Is warm and friendly.
4. Has clear directions, spoken or posted, for the activity.
5. Has clear directions or agreement about available time: limited or open-ended.
6. Is well organized: The opening signals the process that is to follow.
7. Shows content that is to follow.
8. Includes each person.
9. Allows for connections with the group and with at least one other person (except for some skill-building groups).
10. May involve some problem solving or opportunity to expand awareness or knowledge.
11. Provides transition time from previous life activity to this meeting.

An opening exercise that includes these qualities shows adults that they will be in charge of their learning. It also honors preferences for learning through ears, eyes, and bodies.

QUESTION 4

How Can I Design a Meeting to Help Learning Happen?

Warmth, enthusiasm, indirectness, and cognitive organization are the four qualities of an effective teacher of adults. You may say, "I have warmth and enthusiasm, but I'm not sure about indirectness and cognitive organization." You can learn these qualities by thinking about them and practicing them. Build indirectness and cognitive organization into your meeting plans by using the following five steps.

STEP 1: Plan for Indirectness
Indirectness means allowing people to discover for themselves what they need, rather than insisting that they learn what you think is good for them.

There is an old adage about teaching: "First you tell them what you are going to teach them; then you teach them; then you tell them what you taught them." Makes sense? Yes, if you are doing the *direct* teaching—*pedagogy*. This is the way most of us were taught as children. The teacher decided on the goals and the methods, and we "received" the learning.

However, as people mature, they want to become more and more in charge of their own learning and to have leaders who use andragogy rather than pedagogy. Most adults prefer to learn by *andragogy* —the art and science of facilitating adult learning. Andragogy is based on the assumption that both the leader and the learners are capable of making quality contributions and of reaching competent conclusions. It reflects the fact that adults are grown-up people, and that they already have much knowledge and experience. It responds to adults' preference for being in charge of their own learning and to their need for leaders who facilitate that learning process, rather than for teachers who attempt to control both the goals and the processes of the learning. People who prefer learning by andragogy like to learn indirectly, to have an active part in the goal setting and in the process of the learning situation, and to reach their own conclusions. The parallel adage for teaching mature people is:

- First you and they set the goals.
- Then you tell them briefly what you have to offer and how it relates to the goals.
- Next you provide the opportunity for them to explore, to experience, and to share what they have to offer.
- Finally you ask them what they learned.

You are responsible for the teaching and the structure, but you cannot control what people learn, what insights they glean. If you set learning goals for people instead of with people, if you decide what and how they should learn, you discount their ability to learn what they need to learn for themselves. This is patronizing, or "one-up," teaching. If you insist on trying to control the learning, you teach people to give the response you want or to suffer negative consequences. In this case, people either leave or display compliant behavior, and you do not know what personal learnings or insights they may have gained. Their learnings may have been the opposite of the goals of the class.

Example:

Ned wants to learn to manage his time better. When I do direct teaching and try to stay in charge of Ned's learning, I insist that he solve his time-management problem in the way that I believe is best. What Ned may learn is:

• that my way is confusing to him.
• that he still doesn't know how to manage his time.
• that he will do it differently from the way I dictated.

When I do indirect teaching, I use a different set of teaching techniques than I used in direct teaching. *Indirect* does not mean no direction, or laissez-faire, or manipulative leadership; it means leading learning experiences in a way that allows people to discover information and concepts for themselves.

One way to build indirectness into learning activities is to offer options. This encourages people to make discoveries for themselves. I can help Ned identify several learning resources, including other people in the group, and present my solution as one possibility. Ned may not choose the option I want him to, but he will have several possible solutions. Ned will be in charge of his own learning. Ways to set goals for this kind of learning will be discussed in Step 3 in the section on means objectives (pp. 52-54). When you remember that people will discover what is useful for them, not necessarily what you want them to discover, you will be on the road to indirectness.

You can do additional reading about indirect teaching in *The Modern Practice of Adult Education* by Malcolm Knowles.[4] In this book he describes andragogy and contrasts it with pedagogy.

For those of us who have a tendency to fall back into pedagogy, the teacher-directed learning that we experienced in our own school years, thoughtful consideration and practice of the various elements of andragogy can dramatically improve our ability to teach adults. Knowles suggests, among other things, that facilitators of adult learning provide indirectness by:

- offering mutual negotiation of objectives.
- giving adults chances to learn from each other.
- using experiential (doing) techniques as well as transmitting (telling and showing) techniques.
- providing an informal, respectful, collaborative climate.

We have already discussed the importance of seeing, hearing, and doing in learning situations. Next we will examine ways to help adults learn from each other.

Opportunities for adults to help each other can be structured in many ways. Small groups of people can work together in teams or committees. Two effective techniques of collecting information from a large group are the *brainstorm* technique and the *suggestion circle*.

Brainstorm

When the person requesting help seems to be asking for a wide variety of creative, horizon-expanding options, use the brainstorm technique to invite a large number of options and stimulate the creativity of the group.

1. Ask the person to state one problem in a clear, concise way.
2. Ask the group to close their eyes and imagine they are in a time and place where this problem is solved, then to open their eyes and think about possible solutions for the problem.
3. Ask each person to write down five or six possible solutions.
4. Write the first suggestion from one person's list on chalkboard or newsprint. Ask everyone in the room to brainstorm off that idea—to give every idea that she thinks of without evaluating its possibility or practicality.
5. Repeat the first idea from each person's list and as many more as the person requesting ideas wants or as the group wishes to take time for.
6. Give the lists to the listener for evaluation. If she wants help with the evaluation and the group agrees to help:
   a. Ask the listener to set guidelines and ask the group to evaluate each idea in turn. Or,
   b. Group ideas into categories, and select the two or three most valuable ideas from each category.

A brainstorm session takes from five minutes to several hours to complete.

Suggestion circle

When the person asking for help seems to be seeking information about alternative solutions to a specific problem, use the suggestion circle to activate clear thinking and tap the wisdom of the group.

1. Contract with the person to be a listener, to accept each suggestion with no more than a "thank you" response.
2. Ask that person to state one problem in a clear, concise way.
3. Ask someone else to make a written list of the suggestions so the listener can give full attention to listening.
4. Ask the people in the suggestion circle to center their bodies, think carefully for a moment about their possible solutions to the problem, and to each give one high-quality, concise "You could . . ." or "I would . . ." suggestion.
5. When the suggestions have been given, remind the listener to take the suggestions home and decide which to use.

A suggestion circle of twelve people takes from three to five minutes to complete.

STEP 2: Negotiate Ground Rules
You may say, "All right, I will follow the principles of andragogy. I will negotiate goals with participants. I will encourage people to talk with and help each other. I will limit my lectures and films and plan ways people can do things. I will remember to be informal. But how do I assure a respectful, collaborative atmosphere?"

Try using ground rules. Every group follows ground rules or develops group norms, although they may never be spoken. You can use ground rules to help you provide the atmosphere you want. These rules can offer the structure and protection that people need in order to be free to learn. (See p. 48.)

What are the best ways to establish ground rules?
1. Explain the ground rules meaningfully in one or two sentences each.
2. Negotiate ground rules with the group. If there are safety or administrative rules that are not negotiable, at least the group can add other rules that are important to the group members.
3. Post the ground rules—in large and clearly written type so all participants can see them.
4. State the ground rules or refer to them in some way at the beginning of each meeting.
5. Demonstrate the ground rules by practicing them throughout the meeting yourself.

What are these ground rules? Ground rules will differ depending on the group. Ground rules for skill-building or task groups, for example, will often address safety, use, and care of equipment and guidelines for the sharing of that equipment. Planning-group ground rules will cover respectful listening to opinions, methods for evaluating suggestions, and consequences for commitments not completed on time.

"Fine," you say, "I can make rules when the group deals with mechanical skills or products, but what kind of rules would I use in a personal growth group?" Example:

Below is a set of ground rules that are useful in discovery groups and sharing groups that focus on internal growth. Consistently used, these rules provide protection and permission for people to make their own decisions to grow. They assure a safe place for people to try out new behaviors, change their words, consider their attitudes, and think about their underlying beliefs. The rules provide a framework for indirectness. They define people as having worth and protect them from embarrassment if they make mistakes.

Ground Rules

1. Everyone participates.
2. Everyone has the right to pass.
3. All opinions are honored.
4. Confidentiality is assured.
5. Leader stays in a position of respect for self and others.

Think about these sample ground rules and consider how you could use each to provide protection for people to grow. The following list explains the role of each ground rule.

Explanation of Ground Rules

1. The *full participation* ground rule (the assumption that everyone, including the leader, will participate, at least mentally, in each activity) protects the participants from being asked to do something that the leader is not willing to do.
2. The *right to pass* protects each individual, including the leader, from having to speak out, from revealing himself when he or she doesn't wish to do so.
3. *Honoring* each person's attitudes, opinions, and beliefs emphasizes that they have helped him or her make sense out of life and therefore have personal validity. This rule also affirms adults' ability to think and to decide for themselves. In addition, it protects the group from the competitiveness of having to decide who is right or wrong when people disagree.
4. The fourth ground rule of *confidentiality* (or no gossip) provides protections for people to role play new behavior and then decide if they want to keep or discard it. It also encourages people to solve *within* the group those problems they may have with the group, rather than complaining about it to outsiders. Take care to check on whether the group wants to use this rule as the leader has no way to enforce it.

5. The fifth ground rule (that the leader is expected to stay in a position of *respect* for self and others during the meetings) protects the participants from criticism and the leader from loss of integrity. The leader is free to express his or her own belief position but is not to push it on other people or to apologize for it in order to please the group. This ground rule demands that the leader model respectful, accepting behavior for the group. It does not assume that every behavior is all right, but rather that the *needs* of each person are important. For example, the leader will not permit one person to dominate the group with constant talking and questions, but will respect that person's need for attention.

Three of these ground rules *(full participation, right to pass,* and *acceptance for everyone's beliefs)* are borrowed from the methods used in values clarification. If you have not been exposed to these activities designed to encourage people to clarify their own values for themselves, the book *Values Clarification*[5] is a helpful one to start with.

Cognitive Organization

"All right," you say, "I have warmth and enthusiasm. I will design some indirect learning into the meetings, and I will negotiate ground rules to assure a respectful, collaborative climate. But how will I know that I have cognitive organization?" The following three steps address the three essential tasks in cognitive organization:
• Step 3: Set clear behavioral objectives.

- Step 4: Divide the learning experiences into manageable steps.
- Step 5: Arrange the steps to build upon each other in an orderly way.

STEP 3: Set Clear Behavioral Objectives
Objectives are statements about what your group is to accomplish. Whether you call them behavioral, performance, or instructional objectives, the important thing is that they are stated in such a way that you can know whether or not they have been reached.

There are three steps involved in developing measurable behavioral objectives.
1. Select the general goals for your group.
2. Decide whether you will be using ends objectives, means objectives, or both.
3. Identify specific, measurable behavioral objectives.

Select the General Goals

The learning objectives for your group will be based on some kind of needs assessment. In some cases you will have a directive from someone outside of the group.

"Our sales force wants us to develop a course that will teach people who have never used a computer how to enter data into a home budget program."

"The state department of nursing has revised the criteria for certification. We need to be sure we are in compliance."

In some instances you will do a needs assessment and devise objectives within your group.

"My Family Myths and Me Discovery Group"

"Here is a list of categories of family myths we might explore. Read the list. You will notice that it includes general categories like sex roles and holidays. Add any categories that you want to examine that are not included. Then star the six categories in which you are most interested."

"Marriage Encounter Support Group"

"I have a communications questionnaire. Would you like to take it and use the results to help us choose our program focus for the next quarter?"

Choose Ends or Means Objectives

Once the general goals of your group have been determined, you can set measurable objectives. The two kinds of objectives are *ends* objectives and *means* objectives. Ends objectives allow one to measure resulting products and/or participant skills. Means objectives measure the quantity, quality, or diversity of the learning opportunities. Both are written with action words so they can be measured.

Ends objectives

In task or skill-building groups and in planning groups where the outcome is a skill or product, that skill or product should be described in clearly measurable ends objectives.

Examples:

    [SHARING] You are leading a group, "Introducing Quality Circles in Your Business—A Six-Step Method." The outcome is to learn a skill—the use of a specific six-step method. The ends objective is: "Each participant will be able to list the six steps and demonstrate the use of one of the steps in a role-play situation."

    [FRAMING] You are chairperson of "The Governor's Task Force on Families." The outcome is to make recommendations to the governor. The ends objective is: "The combined family policy and the legislative recommendations from every county in the state will be on the governor's desk by June fifth."

These two ends objectives are easily measured. You can tell whether you succeeded or not.

Means objectives
Means objectives are useful where the outcome of the learning situation is up to the individual. Means objectives allow you to measure learning opportunities. Behavioral objectives for discovery and sharing groups often cannot be written in terms of ends, either because you cannot know ahead of time what those ends should be or because they are difficult to measure in a meaningful way.

Examples:

    [SHARING] You are leading a symposium on worker safety. A symposium is a technique for increasing awareness by sharing ideas and presenting a variety of positions or suggestions. How would you write an ends objective on awareness of worker safety?

"At the end of the meeting each participant will want to promote safety"? How would you measure the amount or quality of the "want"? Since a symposium is an awareness-raising or option-offering session rather than a skill-building or planning session, a means (how you present) objective is appropriate: "Each participant will have the opportunity to hear about the history of at least three approaches to worker safety and will have the chance to ask questions about each." That means objective is observable and measurable.

Identify Specific, Measurable Behavioral Objectives

When you write behavioral objectives, decide whether you need ends objectives or means objectives for your group. Then write them, using action words, so you will be able to measure them in a reasonable way at the end of the learning experience.
Example:
   You are leading a group on how to enjoy art. It is almost impossible to write an action-oriented ends objective that will accurately measure enjoyment. Would you say, "At the end of the sessions each participant will have experienced (action) one bushel of enjoyment (not a reasonable measure)"? Or (assuming that smiles indicate enjoyment), would you say, "Each participant will smile (action) at least twenty times during the meetings (may not be a relevant measure)"? Students may tell you that they experienced enjoyment, but that is a personal, inter-

nal experience and difficult for someone else to measure.

Look at this means objective for measurability: "Participants will have the opportunity to explore three different art forms in two ways. Each person will try out oil painting, water color, and clay sculpture (action). The group will visit a museum (action) where each person will view several oil paintings, water colors, and sculptures (action) and hear an art historian lecture about the composition and history of each item (action). Each person will be asked to share with the group what she likes about an art work of her choice." You can see that it is possible to measure these means objectives—these actions and opportunities to enjoy—by observing the quantity and quality of learning experiences offered (reasonable measures).

Example:

Did each of the students participate in all four activities? Did I provide adequate material and environment and a well-trained art historian who delivered a lecture that was relevant to the students' background?

While I must write a means objective about *enjoying* art, I could write an ends objective about *evaluating* art: "Each student will evaluate six paintings for color, form, rhythm, balance, and emphasis (action)." That is measurable, for it measures the student's skill at evaluating paintings according to someone else's idea of the elements that make a painting enjoyable. Acquiring that skill may or may not enhance a specific learner's enjoyment of the painting.

Use Action Words

The following list of action words gives you a variety of direct, measurable words to use in writing objectives.

draw	*identify*
collect	*illustrate*
change	*examine*
change from/to	*compile*
tell	*select*
share	*categorize*
interview	*rank order*
read	*conduct*
discuss	*organize*
write	*develop*
list	*explain*
fill out	*isolate*
select	*design*
find	*evaluate*
acquire	*relate*
obtain	*investigate*
memorize	*analyze*
present	*compare*
prepare	*contrast*
define	*edit*
describe	*invent*

These words describe ends objectives and are easy to observe, as in the following examples:

- "Did the student do the activity?"
- "Did he produce six written evaluations, each addressing the five required elements?"

If you insert "will have the opportunity to . . ." before each action word, you have an easily observable means objective. For example, "Did each student have the opportunity to do the activity that we hope will help her toward the end goal?"

- "Did she experience the act of drawing?"
- "Did she have the opportunity to look at some famous drawings and hear comments about them by a competent art historian?"

Be Sure Everyone Knows What the Goals Are

When you are leading a group that meets more than once, clearly state the specific behavioral objectives for each meeting for the benefit of people who like to experience parts and then fit them together. The way these specific objectives relate to the overall goals of the whole learning experience should also be stated for the people who like to see activities in terms of the whole.

Examples:

"Nuclear Arms Study Group"

"Tonight we will hear three examples of recent European newspaper editorials about nuclear arms (means objective). That will conclude our review of the world press. At our next meeting we will examine the Pentagon recommendations on arms development (relates to overall goals)."

"What Makes Your Quality Circles Work?"

"In this session you will each have the opportunity to compare three ways of organizing the first meeting of a quality circle (means objective). That will conclude the section on introductions of circles; after lunch we will move on to explore implementation practices (relates to overall goals)."

"Flower Arranging Class"

"Tonight each person will make an arrangement using dried flowers (ends objective). We will continue to use the design principles that we have practiced at the last three meetings (relates to overall goals)."

"Task Force on Finding Ways Our School Can Identify and Support Children of Divorce"

"Tonight we will present our reports on the activities already going on in the district (ends objective). You can be thinking about how we will incorporate this information into our recommendations (relates to overall goals)."

Help Individuals Clarify Their Goals

Sometimes when you are negotiating goals in a group, you have to help individuals clarify their own goals. For example, you are leading a support group for parents. Some of the parents are clear and specific about what they want: "I want to learn how to set limits about bedtime and how to succeed in getting the kids to stay in bed." This is a clear end goal, observable and measurable. Either the kids stay in bed, or the kids don't stay in bed.

Other parents are vague at the beginning of the meetings: "I think I'm a soft touch." No way to measure that. Ask questions to help the person be more specific, as in the following exchange.

"Will you give an example, Bob?"

"Yes, I'm worried because my ten-year-old daughter is irresponsible."

"Bob, do you want help with your worrying or suggestions for ways to encourage responsible behavior?"

"I want her to be responsible, and I would like some ideas about how to get her to make her bed."

"Perhaps you could use a list of seven or eight things you can do to encourage your daughter to make her bed?"

"Yes."

This conversation demonstrates a measurable objective—a list of seven things Bob can do.

⟨skill building⟩ In a workshop called "How to Manage a Day Care Center," Charlene says, "I need all the help I can get in learning about management."

"Are you thinking about managing the children's behavior?"

"I suppose we can always use help with that, but I'm not so worried about that part. I get along really well with kids."

"Perhaps you are thinking about organizing the food for snacks and lunches."

"Not so much. I was thinking more about the money. My husband always took care of the income tax, and now that I'm divorced I worry about that."

"We have examples of ways to keep monthly accounts and a handbook on how to fill out income tax forms. Would you like us to go through those with you today?"

"Yes, that might help me."

Other people in the group indicate an interest in record keeping, but want to have a special income tax workshop later in the year. Charlene agrees to that but asks to see the income tax handbook. The specific, measurable means objectives are: "The participants will examine and compare two different ways of recording income and expenditures and can look at an income tax handbook."

Further Help

If you want further help in writing measurable objectives using action words, read Robert Mager's book *Preparing Instructional Objectives*.[6] Lynn Lyons Morris and Carol Taylor Fitz-Gibbon's *How to Deal with Goals and Objectives*[7] offers thoughtful and clear guidance on the difference between ends objectives and means objectives.

STEP 4: Divide the Learning Experience into Steps
The next task of cognitive organization is to divide learning experiences into manageable steps. If you have written clear behavioral objectives for the learning experience, you will have simplified the task

of dividing learning experiences. Unclear goals, on the other hand, make it more difficult to identify small sections of the learning.

Example:
    You have been asked to lead a group on preventing chemical abuse for your school district. You are not sure if it is a sharing group or a task and skill-building group. You don't think it is a planning group because you were not asked to head a task force and make recommendations. But you're confused about whether to make recommendations. You get together a few parents and spend an evening talking about drug abuse. The discussion leaps from one drug-related subject to another. Several people agree that drugs are a problem, that the school should be more effective in stopping drug use. However, since the school administration is not very responsive to parents and the problem seems so complex, the group decides that there is not much point in meeting again.

How might people have responded differently if you had decided it could be a discovery and sharing group and had gone in with these suggested goals?

1. To find out how much chemical abuse there is in this district.
2. To become knowledgeable about the physical effects of the commonly used drugs.
3. To learn what is presently being done in the district to prevent drug abuse.
4. To discover what other districts have done that has been effective.
5. To make a presentation on your findings to the parents of the district.

Manageable steps such as those listed below are the processes (the "how to's") that you will use to reach the goals. Your group could help you decide upon the specific steps. Here is one process suggestion for each goal.

1. Contact the local police department for information on drug-related problems.
2. Invite a local doctor or chemical-dependency counselor who is knowledgeable about the physical effects of commonly used drugs to speak.
3. Interview the principal or counselor of each school in the district to find out what is presently being done to prevent drug abuse.
4. Call the local university's chemical abuse department and ask for a list of school districts that currently offer chemical abuse prevention programs. Contact at least three of those districts for information about their activities.
5. Plan a presentation to make to the parents after sufficient data has been collected and considered.

STEP 5: Arrange the Steps in an Orderly Progression

The final task of cognitive organization is to arrange the manageable steps so that they build on each other and to interrelate them to produce a total learning that is greater than the sum of each of the steps. Choose as the first manageable step the activity on which the others can build.

Some learning experiences are easy to divide. They almost jump into an outline form. If you have a project that seems difficult, try writing each manageable step on a separate 3 x 5 card. Lay the cards out, look at them, and arrange them in different ways. Choose the order that seems most reasonable and ask a colleague to look at it and give suggestions.

For the group on preventing chemical abuse, it is obvious that the preparation of a presentation to the parents would be the last step in the process, because it would be a report on the other steps. The rest of those steps could be done in various sequences, or some of them could be done simultaneously by different people. This would not be true in a skill-building class where one skill depended upon the mastery of another.

If you are familiar with all five steps in the adult learning process and want a spartan method of designing a specific workshop or class, use the planning wheel on pp. 100-106.

QUESTION 5

How Do I End the Group, and How Important Is Closure?

"All's well that ends well" may not always be true, but there is nothing good to be said for sloppy endings. The following suggestions make for good, memorable meetings—*and* groups.

- End on time.
- Do an evaluation.
- End on a positive note.
- Get closure at the last meeting.
- Celebrate your successes.

End on time. That honors everyone, including you the leader.

Remember to do some appropriate evaluation. If the group uses end objectives, evaluate those: "Each of you completed your dried-flower arrangement tonight. Beautiful work." If the group uses means objectives, assess those: "We explored the process of oil painting tonight. Did you enjoy it?"

You could ask each person to make one "I learned . . ." statement or to use resentments and appreciations. Ending meetings with resentments and appreciations is a quick, open way to get evaluation of your leadership and to point out that all needs are important, as are both negative and positive feedback. Listen carefully to each offering. Encourage people to make their responses impersonal. Do not promise to do anything about these statements; you may not be able to!

A specific closing activity is appropriate for discovery groups and sharing groups. A good activity provides a way for people to say goodbye to others in the group and to this occasion, so that they can say hello to the next people and events in their lives.

Check your closing activity for these six items:

1. Has clear directions for the activity.
2. Allows time for clarifying obligations and expectations for follow-up activities.
3. Involves participation from everyone.
4. Allows a way to celebrate new knowledge, insight, or experience with others who were present.
5. Offers each person a time for receiving and giving positive personal messages.
6. Ends on time!

Example:

Your group has talked about traditions: what they

are, how they are formed, and how they function in society. At the end of the meeting you could say, "Does anyone have any questions about what we will be doing at our next meeting? Does anyone have any resentments about this meeting? Any appreciations? For our closing activity, will you please tell at least one other person here one family tradition you are glad you have and one family tradition that you would like to start? Thank you, and good night."

If the group has a series of meetings, do an extensive evaluation at the last meeting. If there were skills or products, involve the group in evaluating those. If this was a discovery or a sharing group and you met your means objectives, but you would like some information on how individuals responded to the process, there is a sample form that can be used or adapted for that purpose on pp. 112-13.

Encourage people to count their personal wins at the final meeting, just as you count your own successes as a leader. Claim the personal growth you made as you moved with the group through these meetings. Count the skills you have achieved as a competent, effective facilitator of adult learning. Claim your warmth, your enthusiasm, your ability to lead indirectly, and your skill at cognitive organization. *Celebrate your successes.*

QUESTION 6

What Is My Responsibility to the Group? What Is My Contract?

Group leaders are generally accustomed to making contracts with their employers or with sponsoring institutions. Some of the following questions might be answered in such a contract: What exchange of money is involved? How is the class advertised? Who opens up the meeting room? Does the leader turn off the lights and lock up? Are refreshments available, and at what price? Who evaluates the leader's work and how?

Leaders also make contracts with their groups. I have attended groups where the only contract that is discussed between a leader and the group members is for the exchange of money. I believe that there are many elements that need to be specified in the contract a leader has with a group. Some of the elements of the contract may be assumed or unstated, but several should be spoken or written.

Overt contract with the group

At the first meeting the leader should review the written or spoken contract (the overt contract) with the group (for an example, see p. 72). If a participant saw a notice of a workshop in the newspaper or read a description of the class in a catalog, that description forms the written contract. The participant expects you to deliver those results.

 If the group is a discovery group, you provide the structure so that people can make discoveries for themselves.

 If you are leading a sharing and support group, you offer ways that people can grow and interact with each other.

 For a skill-building group, you provide the structure for the people to acquire the skills described in the contract.

In a planning group, you help people to construct a way to produce the plan.

Be sure that you have a clear contract with your group—that you and they are there for the same reasons.

Unspoken contract with the group

The elements that are assumed or unstated usually have to do with being ethical and competent. Consider the following lists of possible implicit or unstated items that the leader agrees to abide by in an adult learning group.

Item 1: The leader *provides structure:*

- by doing his homework; by being thoroughly acquainted with the meeting plans, both in content and process.
- by taking charge of the setting: attending to temperature and fresh air, insisting that outside distractions not interfere with the flow of the meetings, arranging furniture so that people are sitting comfortably.
- by managing the mechanics in a way that shows respect for learners: attending to the visual learners with visual aids large enough for everyone to read, to the auditory learners by making sure the acoustics are suitable, to the kinesthetic learners by including movement in the activities; providing any props needed to assist learning.
- by starting on time.

Item 2: The leader *trusts adults to make their own decisions* and avoids telling people what to decide. She also refrains from thinking it essential to know all of the answers. The leader expects to learn from and with the group.

Item 3: The leader provides opportunities for people to learn by offering tools, not by solving people's problems *for* them. Sometimes it is difficult to know whether we are helping people solve their own problems and become more self-sufficient, or simply taking care of people in a way that undercuts their competence and encourages them to be dependent. If you have a question about whether you are helping or are rescuing in a way that invites dependence around a particular problem or skill (Rescuing with a capital R),[8] ask the following questions:

- Did the person ask you for help?
- Did the person work at least as hard at finding a solution as you did?
- Did the person say "Thank you"?
- Did you feel comfortable (not resentful) about giving help?
- Was there a cut-off date on the aid—a time when the person would assume full responsibility for this problem?

If the answer to two or more of the questions is "no," then it's time to refocus on creating a situation where people can solve their own problems.

Item 4: The leader *provides protection for group members* by scrupulously observing the ground rules. The leader is careful to set the rules that are necessary in order to function well as a leader and to provide a climate that is informal, respectful, and collaborative. Working with a team teacher may protect the leader from inviting dependency and from the demands of scheduling. The leader may then have less work and more fun, and even sometimes miss a meeting.

Item 5: The leader contracts *to run a discovery, a sharing, a skill-building, or a planning group, not a therapy group.* (For a longer explanation of this point, see question 8 on p. 88.)

If you think these five items will help you lead your group, use them. If not, rewrite them to better fit yourself and your situation. You must be explicit and clear with yourself about your unspoken contract with the group in order to be a competent, ethical leader.

What is my responsibility to my employer? What is the contract?

Leaders need to be concerned about making a contract with their employers. Often such contracts are not very complete. If the employer says, "Come and do your thing on stress reduction on May 23; we will pay you $_____," and you do it, let's hope that all of the unspoken expectations of both you and your employer will be met. Consider these exchanges:

> You: "I brought my transparencies. Where is the projector?"
>
> Employer: "We expect trainers to provide their own equipment." _____

> Employer: "About that workshop you were doing for us tomorrow—well, not many people have signed up, so we decided to cancel it."
>
> You: "Oh." _____

> You: "How did you like the workshop?"
>
> Employer: "It wasn't quite what I expected." (To his colleagues the employer says, "Don't hire that consultant; he is no good.")

CONTRACT   FORM

Leader

Name **Jennifer Wadely**

Address **1437 15th Ave. S.E.**
Minneapolis, MN 55760

Phone (612) **888-8888**

Service Agreement: **(See back of sheet)**
   (attach sheet)

Date(s): **July 18**
Time: **1:00 - 4:00 P.M.**
Place: **Northland Comm. College, Student Union**
Consideration: **J. Wadely will receive a $ __ fee plus travel expenses.**

Penalty: **If I do not meet my service agreement as evaluated by Matt Simon, I will take a 15% reduction in fee. - J.W.**
Celebration: **I will ask Matt Simon to write a letter of commendation for me.**

Signature **Jennifer Wadely**
Date **January 10**

Employer

Name of Organization __State Environmental Science Assn.__

Address __Rm. 419, Archer Bldg., 59 Central Ave.__
__St. Paul, MN 55773__

Phone (6/2) __111—1111__

Contact Person __Matt Simon__

Address __(same as above)__

Phone ( ) __(same as above)__

Service Agreement: __(See back of sheet)__
   (attach sheet)

Consideration: SESA will receive three
hours of training for high-school
science students & their teachers.
Penalty: If we cancel the workshop
later than April 1, we will pay 15% of the
consultants fee. If we cancel later than
Celebration: July 1, we'll pay full fee. — MS
We'll take the staff to dinner on July 22.
J. Wadely will be invited.

Signature __Matt Simon__

Date __Jan. 14__

The preceding contract spells out the responsibilities of both the employer and the employee. The fact that both reward and penalty items are explicit in the contract indicates that you as a leader are professional and responsible. Note that the celebration item reminds you to count your successes and experience closure with the group. It may also remind some employers of the need to celebrate. The service agreement section of the contract can be brief or very complete, depending on your needs for the specific situation, but should include delivery dates for all goods and services promised.

QUESTION 7

What Will I Do if Problems Arise?

If a problem comes up, identify it; then think and feel what you need to do to resolve it.

Whose problem is it? If it is other people's, go back and renegotiate the contract—you are there to offer tools; it is up to *them* whether or not they use them. If it is yours, you can fix that. Read the sample problems and solutions on the following pages for help with problem solving.

Problem: Group dynamics

• Is the meeting dragging? Speed it up; you, as leader, are responsible for pace.

Is the energy low? Keep the meeting moving. Check the temperature and ventilation; the room may be hot and stuffy.

Are the chairs comfortable? Does the setting encourage alertness? Small chairs or bean-bag chairs encourage bodies to double over, energy to lower.

- Are you working too hard? A leader who tries hard to answer every question discourages other people from thinking independently.

  Are you working with too small a group? You may need more people for greater interaction.

  Or are there too many people? See if you can split up the group for some tasks.
- Are people not talking? Check yourself to be sure that when you ask a question, you make eye contact with several people and then wait for an answer. Follow the ground rules: Insist that each answer be treated with respect, and honor

"passing"—use it yourself sometimes.

- Do one or two people talk all the time or dominate the group with laughter or sarcasm? Do people use group time to try to fix problems that are not part of the group contract? Insist on the use of the ground rules and on sticking to the tasks at hand.

Problem: Time

- Is the group unable to cover the meeting plans in the time allotted? Do whatever works. If the group finishes early, okay. But don't run overtime. Either speed up, ask the group to extend the meeting times, or change the objectives.
- Be clear about whether group activity is on clock time or task time. "We have twenty minutes for this activity" is clock time. "Take as long as you need to finish this activity" is task time. "You must complete this in seven minutes" is clock *and* task time, and is stressful.

Problem: Individuals

- Someone complains that a learning experience is phony, insincere. Remind him of the right to pass. Suggest that he can separate awkwardness and insincerity.

    Someone says, "Why all the exercises? I'm not learning anything. Where is the meat in the course?" Remind her of the right to pass. Remind her that some people learn faster by doing than by lecture. Invite her to read supplementary material.

- Someone says, "Too much theory—I like it when we *do* things." Remind him of the right to pass. Point out that people's learning styles differ, that some people learn more quickly if they grasp theory first. Check yourself to see if you are offering too much theory. Are you thinking for people (spoonfeeding)? Listen for kernels of truth in the complaints, but make your own judgments.

- Someone is *continually* saying, "Yes, but . . ." or "But don't you think that . . ." and pulling the group off on a tangent. Don't even answer "Yes, but's." Get one round of suggestions from the group and then move on. Or invite that person to say what she thinks, honor it, and then go on with the meeting.
- Someone repeatedly stops the group because he is confused. You could say, "It sounds as if part of you wants to believe (or do) one thing and part of you wants to believe (or do) something else." This statement often helps the person focus on what he thinks or wants; then he can decide if he wants to join the group activity.

- Someone is resistant and disrupts the group process. If humor doesn't work, try nurturing. You could say, "I think I know how you feel. It looks as if you don't want to be here. I'll go ahead and lead this group, and you can decide if any parts of it are useful to you. They may be or they may not be."
- Someone criticizes you severely. Do not respond. Explaining and/or defending puts you on the defensive. Saying "I resent your saying that" invites the critic to fight. You are not obliged to make any immediate response to resentments except to listen and think. You could say, "I will think about that." Look for the kernel of truth in the criticism and change your behavior if that is appropriate. Ask for resentments and appreciations at the end of every meeting.
- Someone stays *after* the meeting to criticize what you did during the meeting. She says, "You were awful at first, but I'm glad I gave you a chance. You turned out to be not as bad as I thought. I'll tell you what you should have done instead." If you have asked for suggestions during the meeting or for resentments and appreciations at the end, this type of comment is crooked help. Ask her to bring it up during the next meeting. Then leave. Do not listen to this type of criticism. Make a place for people to give feedback during the meeting, and use it.
- Someone interrupts the group with constant questions. Remember, incessant questions (except from a three- to six-year-old) are a "fight maneuver." You can decide to fight, or you can focus on the

person, get a three-minute round of suggestions from the group in response to one of the questions, and then decline to be drawn into a discussion during or after class.

- Someone pushes you during every meeting. When you fix one thing, he pushes on something else. Some people push. For them, if you fix the whole world, they will push you for not having fixed the moon and the stars. You must choose which pushes to respond to and how much to respond.

Problem: You

- You are scared. Tell yourself you can be scared and lead at the same time. Take care of yourself, and pamper yourself before the meeting. Remember specific instances when you have done clear thinking and good problem solving. Affirm yourself and go ahead.

- You have difficulty accepting personal criticisms or challenges to your leadership. Practice alternative responses at home, and use a response at the meetings that respects both the other person and yourself. Be sincere. Example: Someone says, "I think you are phony when you say you are glad I am here. At the last meeting you didn't act glad."

 Do not take responsibility for the other person's discomfort and offer to change yourself to please her. Do not say "I'm sorry you feel that way, and I want you to believe that I really am glad to see you. I wouldn't say that if I weren't, and if it bothers you that I said that, I will not say anything like that again. I want you to tell me if you are uncomfortable with my words, and I will change them."

 Do not be defensive. Avoid saying "I'm really upset that you feel that way. What can I do to prove to you that I am sincere? Because I really am sincere!"

 Do not attack. Avoid comments like "Well, I'm trying to stay glad that you are here, but it's hard."

 Do not be vindictive. Avoid "Look, it really doesn't make any difference to me whether you think I am sincere or not!"

 Do not placate. Avoid saying "I can see why you would feel that way, and I'm glad you told me. Just stick around and I will try to prove to you that I am glad."

 Do stay respectful of self and others. Say "I accept that you think I am not sincere.

I am, but it is okay with me if you don't believe that.'' And then go on with the meeting.

- You feel the urge to be critical—to send a destructive zinger. This feeling usually comes after some small or large frustrating experience in the group. But good group leaders don't send zingers, so what to do instead?

As a group leader, Charlie tries to be extra nice, helpful, and agreeable, and hide his frustration. However, the frustration often builds, so Charlie feels victimized, and then is again tempted to put someone down. Readers familiar with the *drama triangle* will recognize that Charlie has hit each point on the triangle, an exercise in ineffectiveness and futility.

Drama Triangle

Stephen Karpman invented the drama triangle to give people a tool for realizing when they are engaged in an ineffective series of communications. He identified the three corners of the triangle as *persecutor, rescuer,* and *victim,* with victim at the bottom, because the ineffective dance around the triangle will go on only as long as someone is willing to be victimized.

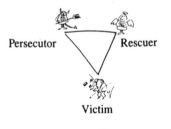

Persecutor   Rescuer

Victim

In our example, Charlie felt victimized by the frustrating events in the group's interaction (victim position). He then considered criticizing (persecutor position) but instead hid his feelings and was extra helpful (rescuer position). Soon he was feeling victimized again.

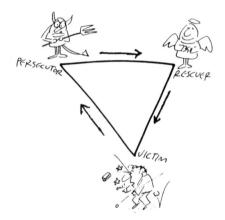

How can we get off the triangle? As soon as we recognize that we are in this vicious triangle, we have clues about how to get off, what to do instead. For example, when Ryan interrupts repeatedly, Charlie can choose the spot from which to move off the triangle.

𝒫 From the persecutor position, move to clear structure.

Persecutor: "Your interruptions are intolerable! You don't have enough self-discipline to choke a fly!"

Structure: "When people are interrupted, they don't get to finish their thoughts. Ryan, please state your position and then we will go around the circle, clockwise, and each give our opinion or pass."

R From the rescuer position, Charlie can move to clear nurturing—taking the needs of the individuals into account.

Rescuer: "I can tell it's too hard for you to wait 'til Martha finishes, Ryan."

Nurturer: "Ryan, if there is something you need from us, we will listen to you as soon as Martha finishes speaking."

V From the victim position, the leader can move to problem solving.

Victim thinks: They are interrupting and we will never get this problem solved and there is nothing I can do.

Problem solver says: "Attention, please! Our meeting is supposed to end in twenty minutes, and we have not resolved the problem. Are you ready to vote on this point now?"

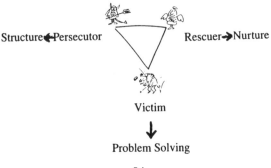

Structure◄Persecutor   Rescuer➔Nurture

Victim

↓

Problem Solving

To practice using the drama triangle, put a masking-tape triangle on the floor; move around it and identify what you, as a group leader, would say and feel at each position. Then practice the three ways of getting off.

These ways of getting off the triangle were first identified by Gail Nordeman. You can read more about the drama triangle in *Born to Win: Transactional Analysis with Gestalt Experiments*.[9]

Problem: Your leadership skills

- You have difficulty getting people to think for themselves. Listen to the way you are inviting them to participate.

 Do not say "Would you. . . ." That is an invitation for the learner to please you instead of thinking for himself.

 Do not say "What I want you to do

is. . . ." That is a worse statement than "Would you. . . ."

 Do not say "Do me a favor. . . ." Worse still.

 Do not say "Could you. . . ." This question implies that the leader doesn't have power.

Do not say "I was just going to say, could you. . . ." This is even more powerless.

Do not say "Why don't you. . . ." That is a secret message that they certainly ought to do something.

Do not say "Now you will. . . ." This is an invitation to rebellion.

Do say "Will you. . . ." It leaves people free to say yes, say no, or pass.

Do say "I invite you. . . ." This offers permission to try out something new.

Do say "I encourage you. . . ." This message offers support.

Do say "If you are willing. . . ." It reminds the person that she is in charge of her own learning.

Do say "Will someone. . . ." This invitation does not put anyone on the spot.

Remember to use these *Do* statements only if "No" is an acceptable answer. Otherwise you are using the question as a crooked way of giving a command.

- You notice that people frequently act confused, ask to have directions repeated more than twice, and seldom complete tasks accurately.

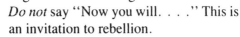 Post clearly written directions.

Tape record yourself giving directions and listen for ways to improve your delivery.

 When you are introducing new content, use a familiar process, and when you are introducing a new process, use familiar content.

 Avoid giving more than three directions at one time.

Problem: Not enough joy

• If you are not having as much fun leading as you want:

 Ask for extra appreciations at the beginning and the end.

 Get a team leader; remember to nurture each other, problem solve together, have fun together. While you are leading, ask each other for help, respect each other's opinions and skills, and interrupt each other with ideas and facts. But do not interrupt in a way that distracts the other person's thinking.

 Remember it is okay to enjoy the people in the group. Honor their knowledge, share yours, learn from them, and laugh with them.

QUESTION 8

What Will I Do If Someone Wants to Use the Group for Personal Therapy?

Is there someone in your discovery group who wants to use the group to solve personal problems? If you want to do therapy (and you are a therapist), stop leading this learning group and start a therapy group. Otherwise, you can refer that person for counseling or therapy. When do you refer someone for therapy? I'm not certain when *you* should, but I can tell you when *I* do. When I observe a person who is exhibiting emotions that seem to be grossly out of proportion to the situation, I tell the person my observations and ask if he or she is interested in getting some help. If the person says yes, I suggest places to go for help. I refer only people who want to change, since therapy doesn't do anything *to* people; it only gives them new tools to do something *for themselves*. I find no point in referring people who want to stay where they are.

If you want to lead a learning or growth group, how can you keep from wandering over into therapy? Since there is some learning in therapy and some therapy in learning, there's not a clear-cut line between them. I use the following five questions to help me differentiate.

1. *How does the group approach the individual's problems or disruptive behavior?* The learning group addresses a problem in a way that furthers the learning goals of the whole group. Example: "Does one of the areas we have been studying relate to that problem?" The therapy group looks for the roots of the problem and how it can be resolved at that level. Example: "When was the first time you had that problem?"

2. *What is the focus of the group activity?* The focus in a learning group is on information or skills the whole group can use. Example: "If you are willing, we can use the criticism you describe as an example. We can all practice some ways to reject destructive criticism." The focus in a therapy group is on how the individual functions. Example: "What benefit do you get out of accepting a criticism like that?"

3. *When is feedback given?* In a learning group, feedback is given when asked for or when it relates to a skill being learned. Example: "Did I

do that correctly?" "Not quite. Try it again and this time. . . ." In therapy, feedback is given routinely. Example: "What is going on with your feet? You have been moving them all of the time you were talking."

4. *What are the primary objectives of the group?* The objectives of a learning group are to acquire new understandings, skills, and behaviors. Example: "You seem to be especially interested in this topic. Do you want us to run through it again with a different example?" The goal of a therapy group is to deal with the individual's personal problems and possibly with his hidden motivations. Example: "When we talk about feelings, you start a conversation about something else. What's going on with you?" Personal behavior change comes from both groups.

5. *How does the role of the leader differ in the two groups?* The leader of a learning group looks for positive areas to build on. Such a group leader functions as a facilitator, focuses on group processes and tasks, directs and coordinates activities, intervenes when behavior interferes with the group tasks, and deals with the here and now. The leader of a therapy group also looks for positive areas to build on, but in addition confronts negatives, focuses on group processes as they affect individual needs, interprets interactions and motivations, intervenes to interpret meaning of behavior, and deals with the here and now *and* the past.

You may note that some people feel a warning, a body tightening, when a learning group is getting into personal therapy issues. I believe that when the leader is certain about the purpose of a learning group, the issue of individual therapy is less apt to surface. Know your purpose and trust yourself.

QUESTION 9

What Can I Do to Prepare Myself?

Who takes care of the leader? *The leader does,* and you can learn to take care of yourself in the following ways.

- Prepare your content carefully, and become thoroughly familiar with your meeting plans. Practice these plans aloud, or meet to review them with a co-leader.
- Take time for yourself. Schedule adequate time for rest, food, and contemplation before the meetings. Remember that poor grooming shows disrespect for yourself as well as the people you work with, so spend some time on your appearance. You deserve it!

- Visualize yourself as the warm, enthusiastic, competent, dynamic leader you are becoming. Get affirmations (positive messages about yourself) before the class. If it isn't possible to get them from other people, make a tape of the messages you need to hear and listen to them before each meeting. Affirm yourself. Write out the affirmations that will help you lead effectively, and say them to yourself five times on the way to the meeting. Affirmations:
    - I am a competent, warm, caring, intuitive leader.
    - I think well on my feet.
    - I listen to what people want and need.
    - I provide firm, but flexible, structure.
    - I am lucky to have this opportunity, and these people are lucky to work with me.
    - I enjoy leading this group.
- Separate your own feelings, thinking, and beliefs. Claim your beliefs, affirm your ability to think, and take care of your feelings. If you feel hurt by criticism from group members, learn to hear the kernel of truth that is in the criticism and use it to improve your facilitating ability. Let the bad feelings go.
- If you are only comfortable with "either/or" answers, practice looking for five possibilities rather than settling for "either/or" solutions.
- If you want a gold star for leading a group where everyone agrees, get help! It is possible to coerce people, but it is often not possible to get everyone to agree. Get a box of gold stars, some stickers, several brass plaques, or some other type of rewards, and give them to yourself freely. You don't

have to earn them by having people agree with you; you have already earned them by your willingness to lead indirectly and to encourage people to come to their own conclusions.

- Be aware that you set the tone for the meeting by your behavior in the first three minutes. Before you enter the meeting, get in touch with your own warmth and enthusiasm, and remember that the class is lucky to have a caring leader like you. You start the meeting from the moment you see the first person. Forget to say negatives like "I don't know if I can do this"; instead say positives like "I'm glad to be here. This will be an interesting session."
- Remember, it is okay to have fun while you lead.

QUESTION 10

How Do I Plan My Meeting?

You have your warmth and your enthusiasm. Now you are ready to do the cognitive organization and to plan some indirect methods of learning.

First, review your *contract*. If you are not sure about it, review Question 6 (What is my contract?) on pp. 67-74. If you don't have enough information, ask more questions. Talk to the person who asked you to lead the group or to someone who will be attending the group, and ask what they expect of you.

Think about what *type of group* you will be lead-ing. Examples of each of the four types of groups (discovery, sharing, skill-building or task, and planning) are offered throughout this book. If you are not sure which type best describes your group, re-read pp. 2-12. If your group is a combination of two or more types, keep that in mind, particularly while you are planning for goal setting and evaluations. Review Step 3 (set clear behavioral objectives) on pp. 27-29. Now make your meeting plan. Use the meeting plan form on p. 118 to record it.

Before each meeting,

- set your *goals*,
- identify your *ground rules*,
- plan the *opening*,
- design the *main learning steps*,
- plan the *closing*,
- prepare an *evaluation*, and
- collect or prepare any needed *materials*.

Reread any of the questions in this book that will help you feel more sure of yourself. Affirm yourself, and you are ready to *go*.

After the group has met, think about how well you led the meeting. Claim your successes. Celebrate the things you did well. Forgive yourself for any things that you did not do well, and decide how to do them better the next time. That's what good leaders do, so go ahead. Do it. You *can* lead a group and you can do it *well*.

HOW TO CONTINUE

Now that you have become an effective group leader, you can continue to improve your leadership skills throughout your life by using the following techniques.

- Take note of things you do that work well and refine those skills.
- Develop an awareness of behaviors that do not work and experiment with other ways of doing those things.
- Observe other good leaders, adapting what they do to fit your style.
- Read about group dynamics and leadership skills to learn new methods.

In Conclusion

I hope the ideas in this book continue to be useful to you. If you have comments about how this information has helped you, or if there are items you would like considered for future editions of this book, you can write to me in care of Parenting Press, Inc. I encourage you to become the good, warm, indirect, well-organized, enthusiastic leader you are capable of being!

Jean Illsley Clarke

NOTES

1. Jean Illsley Clarke, *Self-Esteem: A Family Affair* (Center City, Minn.: Hazelden Press, 1978 & 1998)

2. Nathaniel Lee Gage, *Teacher Effectiveness and Teacher Training: The Search for a Scientific Basis* (Palo Alto, Calif.: Pacific Books, 1972)

3. Allan Tough, *The Adult's Learning Projects* (Toronto: Ontario Institute for Studies in Education, 1975)

4. Malcolm Knowles, *The Modern Practice of Adult Education* (Englewood Cliffs: Cambridge Book Co., 1988)

5. Sidney Simon, Leland Howe, and Howard Kirschenbaum, *Values Clarification* (New York: Warner Books, Inc., 1995)

6. Robert F. Mager, *Preparing Instructional Objectives* (Atlanta: Center for Effective Performance, Inc., 1997)

7. Lynn Lyons Morris and Carol Taylor Fitz-Gibbon, *How to Deal with Goals and Objectives* (Thousand Oaks, Calif.: Sage Publications, Inc., 1978)

8. Claude Steiner, *Scripts People Live: Transactional Analysis of Life Scripts* (New York: Grove Press, 1974)

9. Muriel James and Dorothy Jongeward, *Born to Win: Transactional Analysis with Gestalt Experiments* (Menlo Park, Calif.: Addison-Wesley, 1971)

APPENDIX:

THE PLANNING WHEEL

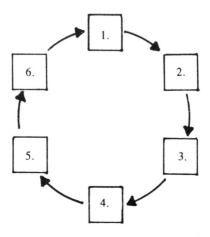

The planning wheel is a six-step method of planning, leading, and evaluating a learning experience. It is a circular method of taking knowledge, behaviors, and values into account as we plan learning experiences. On the wheel, the steps are connected by arrows, representing the values we use in moving from one step to the next. (See p. 104 for an example of a planning wheel.)

When we start to plan a project, workshop, or series of meetings by selecting learning activities, we skip talking about values and jump directly to Step 4 the "plan of action" step. We say something like, "Let's give a workshop and use role play to teach conflict resolution." We may have forgotten that there are underlying values Step 1 and value judgments used to make decisions throughout any planning process. ➧ ➧ ➧ Perhaps we forgot to find out what people want or need Step 2 . We may even have forgotten to decide what it is that we want people to learn Step 3 .

If a workshop that was planned by choosing learning activities does not "go well," it is usually because there was some conflict in values and/or goals of the leaders/participants/employers. Unfortunately such learning experiences are often "evaluated" by asking the question, "How did it go?" as if *it* had taken form of its own magical energy. Instead we should be asking, "What did the participants learn?" or "How well did the leaders lead?" Step 1 . The use of the planning wheel avoids the "how did it go" pitfall.

The planning wheel was inspired by a circular evaluation theory of Edward A. Suchman's.* His theory suggests that unless we reveal to ourselves the values, Step 1 ➧ ➧ ➧ stated or implicit, upon which we are building our learning model, we will run into difficulty with colleagues, participants, or employers when their values differ from ours.

To use the planning wheel, follow the steps listed below.

Step 1 Think through your basic values.

*Suchman, Edward A., *Evaluative Research: Principles and Practice in Public Service and Social Action Programs*. New York: Russell Sage Foundation, 1967.

Step 2 Identify, in a general way, what you hope to accomplish, or what the results of a needs assessment indicate.

Step 3 Identify the specific behavioral outcomes you will plan for. Differentiate between means goals and ends goals.

Step 4 Decide what learning experiences to offer.

Step 5 Do it—lead the workshop, teach the class, run the project.

Step 6 Evaluate the outcome.

Be aware that you made value judgments each time you moved from one step to the next.

Look at the outcome Step 6 in light of Step 1, your basic values, and decide if this is what you really believe, and if this is how you would lead a similar learning experience in the future. If not, think about what changes you would make. If you did not get the expected outcome from Steps 2 and 3, trace back over each step and the connecting value judgments on the wheel with your colleagues and participants to locate where to make adjustments.

If you or the participants came out with satisfactory learnings that are not direct reflections of the behavioral goals, be reassured. That is not unusual for adult learners. They often modify or change goals as they explore. Start with the clearest behavioral goals you can write. Expect that in groups where the task is discovery, sharing, or planning, the goals may change. The use of the planning wheel can help you identify those changes.

"All right," you say, "but I have to lead a workshop and I have never really thought about what my underlying beliefs or values are. I am just doing what my employer asked me to do." Fine. If you don't know what to fill in for Step 1, start wherever you can. You could start at Step 4 and write down what you think you want to do. Then go back to Step 3 and ask, "Since I wanted to do those activities, what was I trying to accomplish?" Go back to Step 2 and ask, "What were the general wishes I had?" Then go back to Step 1 and ask, "What underlying beliefs or values do I have that explain those wishes?" After you have discovered Step 1, redo Steps 2 and 3, and think about the value judgments (represented by the arrows). Then do Step 4 again and see if you still want to use the activities you originally chose. Often when people go through this process, they develop a new action plan that is more directly related to reaching their goals than the original plan was.

For many people, the wheel seems cumbersome at first. After five or six uses, leaders frequently report that thinking through the six steps cuts total workshop design time by 50 to 75%. They also report that it helps them design training that is clear and creative.

Planning Wheel Project Design

The following diagram is a guide to using the planning wheel. If Step 4 is done first, learning theory and value judgments are implied. If Steps 1, 2, 3, 4, and 5 are done in order, evaluation can be built in, not added on.

To begin your planning, fill in Step 1 (the first block). Then write down the value judgment that leads to Step 2. Next fill in Step 2, and continue around the wheel until the steps and corresponding value judgments have all been noted.

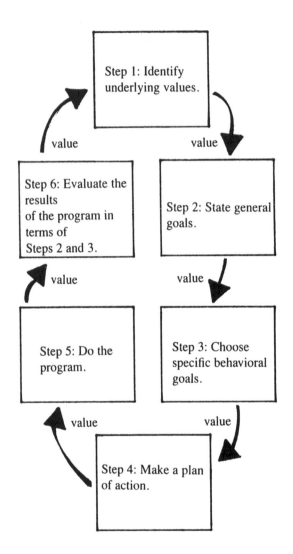

Stress Management
Workshop Design
(Value indicators are underlined)

Step 1: Identify
underlying values.

It is important to be able to manage/<u>handle</u> stress well.

A workshop is a <u>good</u> way to help people <u>learn</u> how to handle stress.   value

Step 2: State general
goals.

People could identify the stressors in their lives and learn some alternative ways of handling them.

People learn <u>better</u> if they experience a few things than if they only heard a lecture.   value

Step 3: Choose
specific behavioral
goals.

Each person will have the opportunity to identify 2 or more stressors, hear recent research, and select ways of handling stressors.

value

Adults

<u>Learn more</u> if they listen, see, and do.

Step 6: Evaluate the results of the program in terms of Steps 2 and 3.

Observe, listen, and give the questionnaires.

It is important to use info from Step b to plan another workshop.

value →

↑ value

Questionnaires at the end of the workshop is a good way to get information.

Step 5: Do the program.

Do the Stress management Workshop.

Think about what might happen if you used these values to co-lead with someone whose underlying value was to help people avoid stressful situations

↑ value

I am a good, competent leader.

Step 4: Make a plan of action.

Identify 2 or 3 stressors and share them, take a fantasy trip to place without stress, hear research; relate the earlier steps; share ways to manage stress.

ABOUT THE AUTHOR

JEAN ILLSLEY CLARKE is an adult educator and a Certified Family Life Educator. She has worked with small groups and large—in the classroom, in the auditorium, before the television camera, and in the radio studio, nationwide and in many countries.

Ms. Clarke has a Master's degree in Human Development and an Honorary Doctorate in Human Services. She is a consultant to human service agencies, civic groups, churches, educational institutions, and businesses. She is the author of *Self-Esteem: A Family Affair,* co-author of *Growing Up Again: Parenting Ourselves, Parenting Our Children* and the *Help! for Parents* books. She is also the trainer and director of an international network of facilitators who use those models in their group work. She edits *We,* a bimonthly newsletter for people who run support groups and other learning groups.

HOW MANY SENSES?

1.

2.

3.

4.

5.

6.

7.

8.

9.

10.

11.

12.

HOW MANY SENSES?

SPEAK   WRITE   move   INTERACT

CONTRACT   FORM

Leader

Name_____

Address_____

_____

Phone (   )_____

Service Agreement:_____
  (attach sheet)

Date(s):_____
Time:_____
Place:_____
Consideration:

Penalty:

Celebration:

Signature_____

Date_____

Permission is given to reproduce this page for group use.

Employer

Name of Organization_____

Address_____

_____

Phone ( )_____

Contact Person_____

Address_____

Phone ( )_____

Service Agreement:_____
   (attach sheet)

Consideration:

Penalty:

Celebration:

Signature_____

Date_____

EVALUATION FORM

1. My expectations for the group meeting were: _____
   _____

2. I learned that: _____
   _____

3. As a result of the group meetings, I plan to change
   my behavior in these two ways: _____
   _____

4. The two group activities or experiences which I
   would rate most valuable are: _____
   _____

5. The two group activities or experiences which I
   would rate least valuable are: _____
   _____

6. The areas to which I would like more attention
   given are: _____
   _____

7. I would rate the group meetings as a whole as:

   ◄──►
     0 1 2 3 4 5 6 7 8 9 10
   poor   (circle one)   excellent

8. Two ways I contributed to the group tasks: _____

_____

9. My participation level for the group meeting was:

$\longleftarrow$ _____ $\longrightarrow$

0 1 2 3 4 5 6 7 8 9 10

passive   (circle one)   very high

10. My goals were/were not met.

            (circle one)

11. Messages for the leaders: _____

_____

CHECKLIST FOR LEADERSHIP SKILLS

Workshop_____
Place_____Date_____Time_____
Facilitator_____

Opening
_____1. Did I start on time? Was the opening warm and inviting?
_____2. Did I negotiate goals or state my goals clearly so others could know if I attained them?
_____3. Did I check expectations of the group? Did I disclaim the ones I could not meet but honor them?
_____4. Did I preview the content and the activities clearly, give the big picture for those who like that security, yet briefly for those who prefer to plunge right in?

Body
_____1. What proportion of time did I "tell" content? (30% or less) What proportion of time did others "discover" content?
_____2. In what specific ways, words, looks, voice, touch, or otherwise did I invite people to be equal with me and with other participants?

_____3. In what ways did I validate people for being where they are and invite them to change if they want to?

_____4. Did I present enough information—and yet not too much?

_____5. Did the participants move or talk every twenty minutes?

_____6. Did I provide for the auditory, the visual, and the kinesthetic learners?

_____7. Did I give sufficient, clear "take-home" material if appropriate?

_____8. Did I like the movement or flow of the workshop?

Closing

_____1. Did I refer back to their expectations/ contracts and honor them? (Evaluation)

_____2. Did I refer back to my own goals? (Evaluation)

_____3. Did I thank people for specific contributions?

_____4. Did I affirm the group at the end?

_____5. Did I end on time?

_____6. Did I end with a higher level of energy than when I started? Did they?

Contracts and Congratulations

_____1. What contracts will I make with myself to improve my workshops in the future?

_____2. How will I congratulate myself and celebrate what I did well in this workshop?

_____3. In what ways did I take care of myself: health, body, working conditions?

CHECKLIST FOR MEETING STRUCTURE

Meeting Design

_____1. Did we set goals together?

_____2. Did I tell them what I have to offer and how it relates to the goals?

_____3. Did I provide opportunity for them to experience and share?

_____4. Did I ask them what they learned?

Warmth and Enthusiasm

_____1. Was I warm and friendly?

_____2. Was I enthusiastic?

_____3. Did I provide a comfortable setting?

_____4. Did I negotiate protective ground rules?

_____5. Did I create a protective climate where it was safe for people to practice new behaviors?

_____6. Did I give the people support for their achievement?

_____7. Did I keep a comfortable pace?

_____8. Did I start on time and end on time with a positive closing experience?

Indirectness

_____1. Did I present the material and then allow the people to make their own decisions?

_____2. Did I invite them to think?

_____3. Did I offer options—to allow the people to discover things for themselves?

_____4. Did I offer ways that the learning experience might directly benefit them?

_____5. Did I structure ways in which the learners could tap the resources in the group?

Cognitive Organization

_____1. Did I state clear behavioral objectives and how they relate to the overall goal of the learning experience?

_____2. Did I divide the learning into orderly steps that built on each other?

_____3. Did I present the theory clearly and point out how it relates to the overall goals?

_____4. Did I offer specific activities that illustrate concrete ways the theories could be experienced in daily behavior?

_____5. Did I offer visual, auditory, kinesthetic, and intuitive learning experiences?

_____6. Were my visuals clear, attractive, and readable?

_____7. Did I respond to questions with appropriate data?

_____8. Was I clear about what I knew and didn't know?

Personal Reflection

_____1. Did I take care of myself by being well prepared? Did I take sufficient time for myself and affirm myself?

_____2. Did I state specifically my responsibility to the group?

_____3. Did I learn with the group?

_____4. Did I have fun?

_____5. What will I do the same/differently next time?

_____6. Did i celebrate my achievements?

MEETING PLAN

Name of group_____

Title of meeting_____

Date_____Time_____Place_____

1. Goals:

2. Opening:

3. Ground rules:

4. Activities:

5. Evaluation:

6. Closing:

7. Materials needed:

8. Affirmations for me to say before the meeting:

INDEX